CLARIFICATIONS

of certain aspects of the

AGREED STATEMENTS

on

EUCHARIST

and

MINISTRY

of the

First Anglican-Roman Catholic
International Commission
together with a letter from
CARDINAL EDWARD IDRIS CASSIDY
President
Pontifical Council for Promoting
Christian Unity

Published for the Anglican Consultative Council and the
Pontifical Council for Promoting Christian Unity

Published 1994 for
The Anglican Consultative Council
157 Waterloo Road, London SE1 8UT

and

The Pontifical Council for Promoting Christian Unity, Vatican City

by Church House Publishing, Church House, Great Smith Street, London SW1P 3NZ

and

Catholic Truth Society 192 Vauxhall Bridge Road, London SW1V 1PD

© The Secretary General of the Anglican Consultative Council and The Secretary of the Pontifical Council for Christian Unity, 1994

All rights reserved. No part of this publication may be reproduced or transmitted in any form or by any means, electronic or mechanical, including photocopying, recording, or any information storage and retrieval system, without permission in writing from the copyright owners.

It is not necessary to seek specific permission for the reproduction of extracts from *Clarifications* amounting in total to not more than five hundred words, provided that an acknowledgement is included as follows:

> *Clarifications of certain aspects of the Agreed Statements on Eucharist and Ministry of the First Anglican-Roman Catholic International Commission* is copyright © The Secretary General of the Anglican Consultative Council and The Secretary of the Pontifical Council for Christian Unity, 1994

If it is desired to make more extensive quotation, application should be made to either of the joint copyright owners.

ISBN 0 7151 4857 5 (CHP)
ISBN 0 85183 929 0 (CTS)

Printed in England by Streetsprinters, Baldock, Herts SG7 6NW

CONTENTS

Members of ARCIC II in attendance at the Venice meeting, 1993, together with Members of the Drafting sub-Committee (Members of ARCIC I)   iv

A Statement by the Co-Chairmen of ARCIC II   1

Clarifications of certain aspects of the Agreed Statements on Eucharist and Ministry of ARCIC I   4

    Eucharist   4

    Ministry and Ordination   8

Letter to the Co-Chairmen of ARCIC II from Cardinal Cassidy   12

MEMBERS OF ARCIC II
in attendance at the Venice meeting, 1993
together with
MEMBERS OF THE DRAFTING SUB-COMMITTEE
(Members of ARCIC I)

Anglican Members

The Rt Revd Mark Santer, Bishop of Birmingham, UK *(Co-Chairman)*

The Rt Revd John Baycroft, Bishop of Ottawa, Canada

Dr. E. Rozanne Elder, Professor of History, University of West Michigan, USA

The Revd Professor Jaci Maraschin, Professor of Theology in the Ecumenical Institute, San Paulo, Brazil

The Revd Dr John Muddiman, Fellow and Tutor in Theology, Mansfield College, Oxford, UK

The Rt Revd Michael Nazir-Ali, General Secretary, Church Missionary Society, London, UK

The Revd Dr Nicholas Sagovsky, Dean of Clare College, Cambridge, UK

The Revd Dr Charles Sherlock, Senior Lecturer, Ridley College, Melbourne, Australia

SECRETARY

The Revd Canon Stephen Platten, Archbishop of Canterbury's Secretary for Ecumenical Affairs

Roman Catholic Members

The Rt Revd Cormac Murphy-O'Connor, Bishop of Arundel and Brighton, UK *(Co-Chairman)*

Sister Sara Butler, Associate Professor of Systematic Theology, University of St Mary of the Lake, Mundelein, Illinois, USA

The Revd Peter Cross, Professor of Systematic Theology, Catholic Theological College, Clayton, Australia

The Revd Dr Adelbert Denaux, Professor, Faculty of Theology, Catholic University, Leuven, Belgium

The Rt Revd Pierre Duprey, Titular Bishop of Thibare, Secretary, Pontifical Council for Promoting Christian Unity, The Vatican

The Revd Brian V. Johnstone CSSR, Professor, Accademia Alphonsiana, Rome, Italy

The Revd Jean M. R. Tillard OP, Professor, Dominican Faculty of Theology, Ottawa, Canada

The Revd Liam Walsh OP, Professor of Dogmatic Theology, University of Fribourg, Switzerland

SECRETARY

The Revd Timothy Galligan, Staff Member, Pontifical Council for Christian Unity, The Vatican

Drafting sub-Committee Members

The Rt Revd Pierre Duprey, Titular Bishop of Thibare, Secretary, Pontifical Council for Promoting Christian Unity, The Vatican

The Revd Jean M. R. Tillard OP, Professor, Dominican Faculty of Theology, Ottawa, Canada

The Revd Christopher Hill, Canon Residentiary and Precentor, St Paul's Cathedral, London, U.K.

The Revd Canon Julian W. Charley, Priest in charge, Great Malvern Priory, Worcester, U.K.

A STATEMENT

by the Co-Chairmen of the Anglican-Roman Catholic International Commission (ARCIC II)

We present here ARCIC's Clarifications of Certain Aspects of the Agreed Statements on Eucharist and Ministry and a letter we have received in reply from Cardinal Cassidy, President of the Pontifical Council for Promoting Christian Unity. These mark a very significant moment in the work of ARCIC and in its reception. Consequently, a few words recalling their background may be helpful.

In September 1981, at the final meeting of the first ARCIC in Windsor, England, the first phase of the Commission's work was brought to a conclusion. This was marked by the publication in 1982 of the *Final Report*, containing all of the first Commission's Agreed Statements and Elucidations. From the beginning, the Commission's method had been determined by the *Common Declaration* between Archbishop Michael Ramsey of Canterbury and Pope Paul VI in 1966. This spoke of "a serious dialogue which, founded upon the Gospels and on the ancient common traditions, may lead to that unity in truth, for which Christ prayed". The method was understood by ARCIC as an endeavour "to get behind the opposed and entrenched positions of past controversies" and the deliberate avoidance of the "vocabulary of past polemics, not with any intention of evading the real difficulties that provoked them, but because the emotive associations of such language have often obscured the truth" (Authority in the Church I, 25). When Pope John Paul II received the members of ARCIC in audience at Castel Gandolfo in 1980 he observed that the method of ARCIC had been "to go behind the habit of thought and expression born and nourished in enmity and controversy, to clothe it in a language at once traditional and expressive of the insights of an age which no longer glories in strife".

By faithfulness to this method, through long, patient and charitable dialogue, in a context of common prayer, ARCIC claimed that it had "reached substantial agreement on the doctrine of the eucharist" (Eucharistic Doctrine, 12); and similarly, on the ordained ministry, a consensus where "doctrine admits no divergence" (Ministry and Ordination, 17). For ARCIC, substantial agreement meant that "differences of theology and practice may well co-exist with a real consensus on the essentials of... faith" (Eucharistic Doctrine: Elucidation).

ARCIC never claimed that its agreement on authority had quite the same quality. What was claimed here was highly significant but more limited: "a high degree of agreement 'on authority in the Church and in particular on the basic principles of primacy'," (Preface to the Final Report). After careful study of the particular issues of papal primacy and infallibility ARCIC spoke of a "convergence" which, taken with its earlier agreements, appeared "to call for the establishing of a new relationship between our Churches" (Final Report, Conclusion). Both Churches have asked the Commission to continue to work on vital issues connected with authority.

From the beginning the Commission recognised that its agreements could not be ratified by the official authorities "until such time as our respective Churches can evaluate its conclusions" (Eucharistic Doctrine, Co-Chairmen's Preface). The ARCIC agreements do not therefore represent the end of a process. Rather, dialogue involves not only a readiness to put questions but also to be questioned. The formal presentation of the Agreements for evaluation, in fact, initiated a further vital stage in the process of seeking reconciliation, during which the appropriate authorities in both communions are called upon to test the adequacy of the Commission's Agreements in the light of their respective faith and practice.

For the Anglican Communion, the Lambeth Conference of 1988 marked a decisive stage in this process. Prior to this all the Provinces of the Anglican Communion had been asked by the Anglican Consultative Council whether the agreements on the Eucharist and on Ministry and Ordination were "consonant in substance with the faith of Anglicans". In asking this question of the Provinces, the Council thus set in motion an official procedure to enable the bishops of the Lambeth Conference "to discern and pronounce a consensus" (ACC, Newcastle, 1981). The responses of the Provinces were officially collated, summarised and published in preparation for the Conference. After noting that the Provinces had given "a clear 'yes'" to these agreements, the Lambeth Conference went on to recognise "the Agreed Statements of ARCIC I on Eucharistic Doctrine, Ministry and Ordination, and their Elucidations as consonant in substance with the faith of Anglicans" (Resolution 8 and Explanatory Note).

After wide consultation and serious reflection, the Catholic Church produced its Response to the *Final Report* in 1991. It spoke very positively of ARCIC's work as "a significant milestone not only in relations between the Catholic Church and the Anglican Communion but in the ecumenical movement as a whole", acknowledging "points of convergence and even of agreement which many would not have thought possible before the Commission began its work." At the same time, concerning the work on Eucharist and Ministry and Ordination for which "substantial agreement" had been claimed, it raised specific issues which "would need greater clarification from the Catholic point of view".

The response of ARCIC to this request is contained in *Clarifications of Certain*

Aspects of the Agreed Statements on Eucharist and Ministry. These Clarifications must, of course, be read in the context of the earlier Agreements or the issues they deal with will appear to be out of proportion. The Clarifications were submitted to the same (Roman Catholic) authorities from whom the request had come. The text is reproduced here, along with the assessment communicated in a letter from Cardinal Cassidy to us as Co-Chairmen of ARCIC. It will be seen that ARCIC's clarifications are judged to have "indeed thrown new light on the questions" so that, as the Cardinal says, "the agreement reached on Eucharist and Ministry by ARCIC-I is thus greatly strengthened and no further study would seem to be required at this stage." These clarifications and the Cardinal's letter constitute a very important element in the reception of ARCIC's agreements on Eucharist and the understanding of Ministry. It is well known, however, that there remains a serious disagreement between the Roman Catholic Church and the Anglican Communion about the ordination of women to the priesthood.

It is our hope that this positive step on the road of reception will assist both communions to recognise that what ARCIC has stated and now clarified does indeed represent agreement about our respective faith and practice. Though much still remains to be discussed, the agreements reached on the important subjects of Eucharistic Doctrine, Ministry and Ordination constitute an important stage in our growth towards fuller communion. We hope and pray that this now more definitive agreement will spur us on to overcoming other difficulties in the way of the full visible unity which our two communions have committed themselves to seek.

+ MARK SANTER
+ CORMAC MURPHY-O'CONNOR
(Co-Chairmen ARCIC-II)

CLARIFICATIONS OF CERTAIN ASPECTS OF THE AGREED STATEMENTS ON EUCHARIST AND MINISTRY OF ARCIC I

In this paper we seek to answer the queries raised in the 1991 Response of the Holy See to the *Final Report* of ARCIC (1982) concerning the Eucharist and the Ordained Ministry (CTS D0609). We are encouraged by what is said in the Response—that this may 'serve as an impetus to further study'.

The Commission was inspired by two official statements of the Roman Catholic Church. The first came from the address by Pope John XXIII at the opening of the Second Vatican Council, when he said: "The substance of the ancient doctrine of the deposit of faith is one thing, and the way in which it is presented is another."[1] The second statement is para. 17 of *Unitatis Redintegratio* which, in speaking of East and West, includes the words, "...sometimes one tradition has come nearer than the other to an apt appreciation of certain aspects of a revealed mystery, or has experienced them in a clearer manner. As a result, these various theological formulations are often to be considered as complementary rather than conflicting." This concept has been endorsed by the *Catechism of the Catholic Church* (1992), which affirms that when the Church "puts down her roots in a variety of cultural, social and human terrains, she takes on different external expressions and appearances in each part of the world. The rich variety of ecclesiastical disciplines, liturgical rites and theological and spiritual heritage proper to the local churches, in harmony among themselves, shows with greater clarity the catholicity of the undivided Church." In our study of Eucharist and Ministry we discovered beneath a diversity of expressions and practice a profound underlying harmony. This harmony is not broken when an element of the truth is more strongly affirmed in one tradition than in another, in which nevertheless it is not denied. Such is especially the case with Eucharistic adoration, as we shall later show.

EUCHARIST

The Response to the *Final Report*, whilst approving the main thrust of the statement on Eucharistic Doctrine, asks for clarification concerning the following points:

a) the essential link of the eucharistic Memorial with the *once-for-all* sacrifice of Calvary which it makes sacramentally present;

---

[1]This quotation is from Pope John XXIII's Italian text. However, the official Latin text in translation reads: 'For the deposit of faith, or the truths which are contained in our venerable doctrine, are one thing, and the way in which they are expressed is another, with, however, the same sense and meaning.'

b) "the propitiatory nature of the eucharistic sacrifice, which can be applied also to the deceased". The Response stressed the fact that "for Catholics the whole Church must include the dead". It appears to want reassurance that the Anglican communion shares the same view;

c) certitude that Christ is present sacramentally and substantially when "under the species of bread and wine these earthly realities are changed into the reality of his Body and Blood, Soul and Divinity";

d) the adoration of Christ in the reserved sacrament.

The Response of the Holy See states that the Catholic Church rejoices because the members of the Commission were able to affirm together "that the eucharist is a sacrifice in the sacramental sense, provided that it is clear that this is not a repetition of the historical sacrifice". In the mind of the Commission the making present, effective and accessible of the unique historic sacrifice of Christ does not entail a repetition of it. In the light of this the Commission affirms that the belief that the eucharist is truly a sacrifice, but in a sacramental way, is part of the eucharistic faith of both our communions. As has been stated in the Elucidation on Eucharistic Doctrine 5: "The Commission believes that the traditional understanding of sacramental reality, in which the once-for-all event of salvation becomes effective in the present through the action of the Holy Spirit, is well expressed by the word *anamnesis*. We accept this use of the word which seems to do full justice to the semitic background. Furthermore it enables us to affirm a strong conviction of sacramental realism and reject mere symbolism".

When we speak of the death of Christ on Calvary as a sacrifice, we are using a term to help explain the nature of Christ's self-offering, a term which is not exhaustive of the significance of that self-offering. However, it has become normative for the Christian tradition because of its intimate relation with the unique propitiatory character of the death of Christ. This theme of propitiatory sacrifice is clearly emphasised in the classical eucharistic liturgies of the churches of the Anglican Communion (e.g. the *English Book of Common Prayer*, 1662), where the words immediately preceding the *Sursum Corda* have always included 1 John 2:1,2, "If anyone sin, we have an advocate with the Father, Jesus Christ the righteous, and he is the propitiation for our sins". So the Prayer of Consecration begins:

> "Almighty God, our heavenly Father, who of thy tender mercy didst give thine only Son Jesus Christ to suffer death upon the Cross for our redemption; who made there (by his one oblation of himself once offered) a full, perfect, and sufficient sacrifice, oblation, and satisfaction, for the sins

of the whole world; and did institute, and in his holy Gospel command us to continue, a perpetual memory of that his precious death, until his coming again..."

Similarly, the propitiatory dimension of the eucharist is explicit in the *Final Report* when it says that through the eucharist "the atoning work of Christ on the cross is proclaimed and made effective" and the Church continues to "entreat the benefits of his passion on behalf of the whole Church". This is precisely what is affirmed at the heart of the eucharistic action in both classical and contemporary Anglican liturgies (eg *The Book of Common Prayer*, 1662):

"O Lord and heavenly Father, we thy humble servants entirely desire thy fatherly goodness mercifully to accept this our sacrifice of praise and thanksgiving, most humbly beseeching thee to grant, that by the merits and death of thy Son Jesus Christ, and through faith in his blood, we and *all thy whole Church* may obtain remission of our sins, and all other benefits of his passion."[2]

'All thy whole Church' must be understood in the light of the article in the Nicene Creed which precedes it, "I believe in the one holy catholic and apostolic church ... in the resurrection of the dead and the life of the world to come". For this reason commemoration of the faithful departed has continued to be part of the intercessions in Anglican eucharistic liturgies past and present (compare also the liturgical provision for a eucharist at a Funeral and in the Commemoration of the Faithful Departed in the *Alternative Service Book*, 1980, of the Church of England, pp. 328ff, 834ff and 936ff).

The Holy See's Response gladly recognises our agreement with regard to the real presence of Christ: "Before the eucharistic prayer, to the question 'What is that?', the believer answers: 'It is bread'. After the eucharistic prayer to the same question he answers: 'It is truly the body of Christ, the Bread of Life'. It also acknowledges that, 'The affirmations that the eucharist is the 'Lord's real gift of himself to his Church' (*Eucharistic Doctrine*, 8), and that bread and wine 'become' the body and blood of Christ (*Eucharistic Doctrine*, Elucidation, 6) can certainly be interpreted in conformity with catholic faith". It only asks for some clarification to remove any ambiguity regarding the mode of the real presence. The Response speaks of the earthly realities of bread and wine being changed

---

[2] A nuanced example of propitiatory language in association with the eucharist is found in the writings of the seventeenth century Anglican divine, Jeremy Taylor: "It follows then that the celebration of this sacrifice be, in its proportion, an instrument of applying the proper sacrifice to all the purposes for which it was first designed. It is ministerially, and by application, an instrument propitiatory: it is eucharistical; it is an homage and an act of adoration, and it is impetratory, and obtains for us and for the whole church, all the benefits of the sacrifice, which is now celebrated and applied; that is, as this rite is the remembrance and ministerial celebration of Christ's sacrifice, so it is destined to do honour to God... to beg pardon, blessings, and supply all of our needs." (Discourse XIX, 4).

into "the reality of his Body and Blood, Soul and Divinity". In its preparatory work the Commission examined with care the definition of the Council of Trent (DS 1642, 1652), repeated in the *Catechism of the Catholic Church* (1992) (No 1376). Though the Council of Trent states that the Soul and Divinity of Christ are present with his body and blood in the eucharist, it does not speak of the conversion of the earthly realities of bread and wine into the Soul and Divinity of Christ (DS 1651). The presence of the Soul is by natural *concomitantia* and the Divinity by virtue of the hypostatic union. The Response speaks of the 'substantial' presence of Christ, maintaining that this is the result of a substantial change in the elements. By its footnote on transubstantiation the Commission made clear that it was in no way dismissing the belief that "God, acting in the eucharist, effects a change in the inner reality of the elements" ... and that a mysterious and radical change takes place. Paul VI in *Mysterium Fidei* (AAS 57, 1965) did not deny the legitimacy of fresh ways of expressing this change even by using new words, provided that they kept and reflected what transubstantiation was intended to express. This has been our method of approach. In several places the *Final Report* indicates its belief in the presence of the living Christ truly and really in the elements. Even if the word 'transubstantiation' only occurs in a footnote, the *Final Report* wished to express what the Council of Trent, as evident from its discussions, clearly intended by the use of the term.

Reservation of the Blessed Sacrament is practised in both our churches for communion of the sick, the dying and the absent. The fear expressed in the Response that a real consensus between Anglicans and Roman Catholics is lacking concerning the adoration of Christ's sacramental presence requires careful analysis. Differences in practice do not necessarily imply differences in doctrine, as can be seen in the case of East and West. The difficulty is not with reservation of the sacrament but with the devotions associated with it which have grown up in the Western Church since the twelfth century outside the liturgical celebration of the eucharist. To this day these devotions are not practised in the Eastern Churches, just as they had not been during the Church's first thousand years. Nevertheless, the belief concerning Christ's presence has been and remains the same in East and West. Obviously the distinction between faith and practice is especially pertinent here. We recognised the fact that some Anglicans find difficulty with these devotional practices because it is feared that they obscure the true goal of the sacrament. However, the strong affirmation that "the Christ whom we adore in the Eucharist is Christ glorifying the Father" (Elucidations, 8) clearly shows that in the opinion of the authors of the document there need be no denial of Christ's presence even for those who are reluctant to endorse the devotional practices associated with the adoration of Christ's sacramental presence. Provision for the reservation of the

Sacrament is found within the Anglican Church according to pastoral circumstances. In the Church of England, for example, this is regulated by the faculty jurisdiction of the diocesan bishop.

The 1662 *Book of Common Prayer* authoritatively expresses the historical Anglican teaching that the consecrated elements are to be treated with reverence. After communion the rubric instructs the minister to "return to the Lord's Table, and reverently place upon it what remaineth of the consecrated Elements, covering the same with a fair linen cloth". A further rubric states that "the Priest... shall, immediately after the Blessing, reverently eat and drink the same". Such reverence remains the Anglican attitude, as can be seen from the collect provided for the Thanksgiving for the Institution of Holy Communion:

> "Almighty and heavenly Father, we thank you that in this wonderful sacrament you have given us the memorial of the passion of your Son Jesus Christ. Grant us so to reverence the sacred mysteries of his body and blood, that we may know within ourselves and show forth in our lives the fruits of his redemption; who is alive and reigns with you and the Holy Spirit, one God, now and for ever."[3]

MINISTRY AND ORDINATION

The Holy See's Response acknowledged that 'significant consensus' has been achieved with regard to Ministry and Ordination. Encouraged by this we seek to give the requested clarifications.
Concerning the Ordained Ministry the Response asks ARCIC to make clearer the following affirmations:

a) only a validly ordained priest, acting "in the person of Christ", can be the minister offering "sacramentally the redemptive sacrifice of Christ" in the Eucharist;
b) the institution of the sacrament of orders, which confers the priesthood of the New Covenant, comes from Christ. Orders are not "a simple ecclesiastical institution";
c) the "character of priestly ordination implies a configuration to the priesthood of Christ";
d) the apostolic succession in which the unbroken lines of episcopal succession and apostolic teaching stand in causal relationship to each other.

Crucial to the ARCIC agreement is the recognition that the ordained ministry

[3]cf. *Alternative Service Book*, 1980, p.920

is an essential element of the Church and that it is only the episcopally ordained priest who presides at the eucharist (*Ministry and Ordination*, Elucidations, 2). In several instances the *Final Report* states that the celebration of the eucharist is the sacramental memorial of the once-for-all self-offering of Christ on the cross to his Father (as described above). In the celebration of the eucharistic memorial, the self-offering of Christ is made present. The community, gathered around the ordained minister who presides in Christ's name at the celebration, enters into communion with this self-offering. In reciting the narrative of the institution, in praying the Father to send the Holy Spirit to effect the transformation of the gifts and through them of the faithful, in distributing these holy gifts to the assembly, the presiding minister stands in a special sacramental relation to what Christ himself did at the Last Supper, pointing to his redemptive sacrifice on the cross. Together with the assembly, but exercising his own specific ecclesial function, the one who presides is thus the minister of the sacramental self-offering of Christ.

The Response seeks the amplification and completion of that part of the *Final Report* which we have just clarified by affirming that Christ himself instituted the sacrament of Orders. Concerning ordained ministers the *Final Report* states, "Not only is their vocation from Christ but their qualification for exercising such a ministry is the gift of the Spirit" (*Ministry and Ordination*, 14), received in and through the Church. In this way they carry on the commission given to the apostles by Jesus in person. After the resurrection the Holy Spirit conferred upon the apostolic group what was necessary for the accomplishment of their commission. They in turn were led by the Lord to choose collaborators and successors who, through the laying on of hands, were endowed with the same gift of God for ministry in the Church.

Thus the sacramental ministry is something positively intended by God and derives from the will and institution of Jesus Christ. This does not necessarily imply a direct and explicit action by Jesus in the course of his earthly life. A distinction needs to be drawn between what Jesus is recorded as saying and doing, and his implicit intentions which may not have received explicit formulation till after the Resurrection, either in words of the risen Lord himself or through his Holy Spirit instructing the primitive community.

> "All this I have spoken while still with you. But the Counsellor, the Holy Spirit, whom the Father will send in my name, will teach you all things and will remind you of everything I have said to you". (John 14:25,26).

The *Final Report* had no intention of excluding the notion of sacramental 'character' which is found in official Anglican documents (e.g. the Canon Law of the Church of England, c.1.2). The Commission believed it to be more constructive to retain the idea without the use of a term which has sometimes been misconstrued. The *Final Report* emphasises the Spirit's seal and the irrevocability of the gifts and calling of God of ministers. This is the meaning of 'character' as described by Augustine, assumed in the Council of Trent (DS 1767, 1774) and taught in the *Catechism of the Catholic Church* (1992) (1582). Thus the *Final Report* states:

> "In this sacramental act, the gift of God is bestowed upon the ministers, with the promise of divine grace for their work and for their sanctification; the ministry of Christ is presented to them as a model for their own; and the Spirit seals those whom he has chosen and consecrated. Just as Christ has united the Church inseparably with himself, and as God calls all the faithful to lifelong discipleship, so the gifts and calling of God to the ministers are irrevocable. For this reason, ordination is unrepeatable in both our churches" (*Ministry and Ordination*, 15).

Anglicans and Roman Catholics agree that the communion of the churches in the apostolic tradition involves not only all the existing churches of today but also those of the past, extending back to the first apostolic community. This communion is rooted in the apostolic faith and mission, but it involves far more than this. The sacramentality of the Church requires a sacramental continuity, expressed especially in the eucharist, celebrated in communion with the bishop:

> "The communion of the churches in mission, faith, and holiness, through time and space, is thus symbolised and maintained in the bishop" (*Ministry and Ordination*, 16).

The prime function of the episcopal ministry is to safeguard the continuity of the local churches with the apostolic Church in its faith, teaching and mission. Thus each episcopal ordination is part of a successive line which links the bishops of today with the apostolic ministry. We believe that this is precisely what *Lumen Gentium* wanted to express:

> "Among those various ministries which, as tradition witnesses, were exercised in the Church from the earliest times, the chief place belongs to the office (*munus*) of those who, appointed to the episcopate in a sequence running back to the beginning, are the ones who pass on the apostolic seed. Thus, as Saint Irenaeus testifies, through those who were appointed bishops by the apostles, and through their successors down to our own time, the

apostolic tradition is manifested and preserved throughout the world". (*Lumen Gentium*, 20)[4]

The Commission stated that its concern was the origin and nature of the ordained ministry, not the question of who can or cannot be ordained (*Ministry and Ordination*, Elucidation, 5). However, the Response maintains that the Ordination of Women 'affects' the *Final Report*'s claim to have reached substantial agreement on Ministry and Ordination. We are confronted with an issue that involves far more than the question of ministry as such. It raises profound questions of ecclesiology and authority in relation to Tradition. This subject is part of the mandate entrusted to ARCIC II.

[September 1993]

---

[4] Inter varia illa ministeria quae inde a primis temporibus in ecclesia exercentur, teste traditione, praecipuum locum tenet munus illorum qui, in episcopatum constituti per successionem ab initio decurrentem, apostolici seminis traduces habent. Ita, ut testatur S.Irenaeus, per eos qui ab apostolis instituti sunt episcopi et successores eorum usque ad nos, traditio apostolica in toto mundo manifestatur et custoditur.

PONTIFICIUM CONSILIUM
AD CHRISTIANORUM UNITATEM FOVENDAM   *E Civitate Vatticana, die* March 11th, 1994

PROT. N.......
1278/94/e

To the Co-Chairmen of ARCIC-II

Bishop Mark SANTER   Bishop Cormac MURPHY-O'CONNOR
Bishop of Birmingham   Bishop of Arundel and Brighton

On September 4th last, you sent me a document containing "Clarifications of certain aspects of the Agreed Statements on Eucharist and Ministry" which had been submitted to and approved by the ARCIC-II meeting taking place in Venice at that time.

This document has been examined by the appropriate dicasteries of the Holy See and I am now in a position to assure you that the said clarifications have indeed thrown new light on the questions concerning Eucharist and Ministry in the Final Report of ARCIC-I for which further study had been requested.

The Pontifical Council for Promoting Christian Unity is therefore most grateful to the members of ARCIC-II, and to those from ARCIC-I who prepared these clarifications. The agreement reached on Eucharist and Ministry by ARCIC-I is thus greatly strengthened and no further study would seem to be required at this stage.

There is one observation that I should like to bring to your notice in this connection. It concerns the question of *Reservation of the Blessed Sacrament*, and in particular the comparison which is made on page 4 of the Clarifications between the practice of the Orthodox Churches (and the Catholic Churches of Eastern Rite) and that of the Anglican Communion. Orthodox and Eastern-rite Catholics have a very clear and uniform practice concerning the reservation of the Blessed Sacrament. While there are differences in respect to devotions connected with the Reserved Sacrament, adoration of the Reserved Sacrament is normal for both Orthodox and Greek-Catholics. The Clarifications do not seem to make clear that this can be said unreservedly and uniformly for Anglicans. In fact the Clarifications state that "provision for the reservation of the Sacrament is found within the Anglican Church according to pastoral circumstances" and that "in the Church of England, for example, this is regulated by the faculty jurisdiction of the diocesan bishop". It seems important to stress that the Response of the Holy See to the Final Report was concerned not with the question of devotions associated with Christ's presence in the Reserved Sacrament, but with the implications of diverse Anglican practice regarding Reservation itself and attitudes towards the Reserved Sacrament.

The remarkable consensus reached up to now on the themes dealt with by ARCIC-I will only be able to be seen in its full light and importance as the work of ARCIC-II proceeds. This would appear to be particularly the case in respect of the study of the questions still open in relation to the third part of the Final Report of ARCIC-I, dealing with Authority in the Church. It would seem urgent, then, that this question be taken up as soon as possible by ARCIC-II.

With the expression of my deep esteem and kind personal greetings,

Yours sincerely in the Lord,

Edward Idris Cardinal Cassidy
President